To:

_____

From:

_____

May the God of hope fill you with all
joy and peace as you trust in him,
so that you may overflow with hope
by the power of the Holy Spirit.

ROMANS 15:13

Footprints
Copyright ©2003 by Margaret Fishback Powers
ISBN 0-310-80309-8

Requests for information should be addressed to:
    Inspirio, The gift group of Zondervan
    Grand Rapids, Michigan 49530
    http://www.inspiriogifts.com

Written by: Margaret Fishback Powers
Compiler: Molly C. Detweiler
Design: Mark Veldheer

Printed in China
03 04 05/HK/ 4 3 2 1

footprints

Reflections on the Best-loved Poem

inspirio™

footprints

One night I dreamed a dream.

I was walking along the beach with my Lord.

Across the dark sky flashed scenes from my life.

For each scene, I noticed two sets of

footprints in the sand,

One belonging to me and one to my Lord.

When the last scene of my life shot before me

I looked back at the footprints in the sand

and to my surprise,

I noticed that many times along the

path of my life

There was only one set of footprints.

I realized that this was at the

lowest and saddest times of my life.

This always bothered me and I questioned

the Lord about my dilemma.

"Lord, you told me when I decided to follow You,

You would walk and talk with me all the way.

But I'm aware that during the most

troublesome times of my life

There is only one set of footprints.

I just don't understand why,

when I needed You most, You leave me."

He whispered, "My precious child,

I love you and will never leave you,

never, ever, during your trials and testings.

When you saw only one set of footprints

It was then that I carried you."

God is With Us...
In Our Dreams

One night I dreamed a dream.

We should not ignore our dreams.
God will sometimes use our
dreams to assure us of his promises
or to tell us something about
himself. And when God does
speak to us in dreams, he will also
help us understand them.

"I will pour out my Spirit on all people.
Your sons and daughters will prophesy,
 your old men will dream dreams,
 your young men will see visions," says the LORD.

Joel 2:28

The LORD appeared to Solomon during the night in a dream, and God said, "Ask for whatever you want me to give you."

Solomon answered, "You have shown great kindness to your servant, my father David, because he was faithful to you and righteous and upright in heart. You have continued this great kindness to him and have given him a son to sit on his throne this very day.

"Now, O LORD my God, you have made your servant king in place of my father David. But I am only a little child and do not know how to carry out my duties. Your servant is here among the people you have chosen, a great people, too numerous to count or number. So give your servant a discerning heart to govern your people and to distinguish between right and wrong. For who is able to govern this great people of yours?" The Lord was pleased that Solomon had asked for this.

1 Kings 3:5–10

God is With Us…
In Our Daily Walk

I was walking along the beach with my Lord.

Health professionals suggest that people who want to become physically fit should try a consistent program of walking. Sustained walking several times a week will improve your muscle tone and strengthen your heart. The Bible reassures us that our spiritual lives will also reap benefits when we are consistent in walking with the Lord.

Those who hope in the LORD
   will renew their strength.
They will soar on wings like eagles;
   they will run and not grow weary,
   they will walk and not be faint.

Isaiah 40:31

This is what the LORD says:

"Stand at the crossroads and look;
   ask for the ancient paths,
ask where the good way is, and walk in it,
   and you will find rest for your souls."

Jeremiah 6:16

God has said: "I will live with them and walk
among them, and I will be their God, and they
will be my people."

2 Corinthians 6:16

Whether you turn to the right or to the left, your
ears will hear a voice behind you, saying "This is
the way; walk in it."

Isaiah 30:21

Come, let us go up to the mountain of the LORD,
  to the house of the God of Jacob.
He will teach us his ways,
  so that we may walk in his paths.

Isaiah 2:3

Your love is ever before me, LORD,
  and I walk continually in your truth.

Psalm 26:3

I will walk among you and be your God, and you
will be my people.

Leviticus 26:12

I guide you in the way of wisdom
  and lead you along straight paths.
When you walk, your steps will not be hampered;
  when you run, you will not stumble.

Proverbs 4:11–12

If we walk in the light, as God is in the
  light, we have fellowship with one
  another, and the blood of Jesus, his Son,
  purifies us from all sin.

1 John 1:7

Blessed are those who have learned
     to acclaim you,
  who walk in the light of your presence,
     O LORD.

Psalm 89:15

If the LORD delights in a man's way,
  he makes his steps firm;
though he stumble, he will not fall,
  for the LORD upholds him with his hand.

Psalm 37:23–24

A joyful heart is the mark of one who has a consistent walk with the Lord, who follows in the footsteps of the Master. Take strength then, and be blessed in a close walk with the Lord, for...

"I will strengthen them in the LORD
  and in his name they will walk,"
    declares the LORD.

Zechariah 10:12

God is With Us...
In the Hard Times

*Across the dark sky flashed
scenes from my life.*

We all go through times when life seems
to overwhelm us. The Bible reassures
us that God's presence is with us to help
us, even when we don't realize it.
Moments of darkness in our lives are
inevitable, but there is hope for all of us.
There is light. Jesus Christ, the Son of
God, is our hope and light in darkness.

God is our refuge and strength,
    an ever-present help in trouble.
    Therefore we will not fear, though the earth
        give way
and the mountains fall into the heart of the sea,
though its waters roar and foam
    and the mountains quake with their surging.

Psalm 46:1–3

You are my hiding place, LORD;
    you will protect me from trouble
    and surround me with songs of deliverance.

Psalm 32:7

Even though I walk
    through the valley of the shadow of death,
I will fear no evil,
    for you are with me, O LORD;
your rod and your staff,
    they comfort me.

Psalm 23:4

Jesus said, "I am the light of the world. Whoever
follows me will never walk in darkness, but will
have the light of life."

John 8:12

God is With Us…
As Our Companion

For each scene, I noticed two sets of footprints in the sand, one belonging to me and one to my Lord.

Wherever we go, we cannot step outside the boundaries of God's love and care. We can have fellowship "with the Father and with his Son, Jesus Christ" wherever we are (1 John 1:3). All we need to do is trust in God's loving companionship and walk the path he has placed before us.

Jesus said, "Greater love has no one than this, that he lay down his life for his friends.... I no longer call you servants, because a servant does not know his master's business. Instead, I have called you friends, for everything that I learned from my Father I have made known to you."

John 15:13, 15

There is a friend who sticks closer than a brother.

Proverbs 18:24

"Can a mother forget the baby at her breast
    and have no compassion on the child she
        has borne?
Though she may forget,
    I will not forget you!
See, I have engraved you on the palms of my
        hands," says the LORD.

Isaiah 49:15–16

Jesus said, "Surely I am with you always, to the very end of the age."

Matthew 28:20

The LORD himself goes before you and will be with you; he will never leave you nor forsake you. Do not be afraid; do not be discouraged.

Deuteronomy 31:8

This is what the LORD says:
"In the time of my favor I will answer you,
  and in the day of salvation I will help you."

Isaiah 49:8

God has said,
  "Never will I leave you;
    never will I forsake you."
So we say with confidence,
  "The LORD is my helper; I will not be afraid.
    What can man do to me?"

Hebrews 13:5–6

Praise the LORD, O my soul,
  and forget not all his benefits—
who forgives all your sins
  and heals all your diseases,
who redeems your life from the pit
  and crowns you with love and compassion,
who satisfies your desires with good things
  so that your youth is renewed like the eagle's.

Psalm 103:2–5

Though it sometimes seems that the whole world has gone wrong around us, we are not alone—God is with us! The awareness of God's presence is encouraging and heartwarming.

So do not fear, for I am with you;
    do not be dismayed, for I am your God.
I will strengthen you and help you;
    I will uphold you with my righteous right hand.

Isaiah 41:10

Jesus said, "I will not leave you as orphans; I will come to you."

John 14:18

The eternal God is your refuge,
    and underneath are the everlasting arms.

Deuteronomy 33:27

How great is your goodness,
    which you have stored up for those who fear you,
which you bestow in the sight of men
    on those who take refuge in you, LORD.

Psalm 31:19

God is With Us...
Never Look Back—
No Regrets!

When the last scene of my life shot before me, I looked back at the footprints in the sand.

When we live with an attitude that looks back over our lives with regrets and "if onlys" we rob ourselves of hope. We rob ourselves of the joy of God's grace. God never changes. He is the God of grace. He is the God of hope. He is the God of love who offers us a life free of regrets.

God has delivered us from such a deadly peril, and he will deliver us. On him we have set our hope that he will continue to deliver us.

2 Corinthians 1:10

If anyone is in Christ, he is a new creation; the old has gone, the new has come!

2 Corinthians 5:17

We know that in all things God works for the good of those who love him, who have been called according to his purpose.

Romans 8:28

There is surely a future hope for you,
    and your hope will not be cut off.

Proverbs 23:18

I have fought the good fight, I have finished the race, I have kept the faith. Now there is in store for me the crown of righteousness, which the Lord, the righteous Judge, will award to me on that day.

2 Timothy 4:7–8

Surely goodness and love will follow me
    my all the days of my life,
and I will dwell in the house of the LORD
    forever.

Psalm 23:6

God is With Us…
In Our Loneliness

There was only one set
of footprints.

God is always with us—in our
joy and in our pain, in the good
times, and in the bad times. His
steadfast love and faithfulness are
promises we can cling to,
promises to bring us joy when we
face loneliness.

Turn to me and be gracious to me, LORD,
    for I am lonely and afflicted.
The troubles of my heart have multiplied;
    free me from my anguish.
Look upon my affliction and my distress
    and take away all my sins....
Guard my life and rescue me;
    let me not be put to shame, for I take refuge
        in you.
May integrity and uprightness protect me,
    because my hope is in you.

Psalm 25:16–18, 20–21

I have set the LORD always before me.
    Because he is at my right hand,
    I will not be shaken.
Therefore my heart is glad and my tongue rejoices;
    my body also will rest secure.

Psalm 16:8–9

Be strong and courageous. Do not be afraid or
terrified...for the LORD your God goes with you;
he will never leave you nor forsake you.

Deuteronomy 31:6

I am always with you, LORD;
    you hold me by my right hand.

Psalm 73:23

God is With Us...
In Our Sorrow

I realized that this was at the lowest and saddest times of my life.

Though things may seem hopeless, "God, who has called you into fellowship with his Son Jesus Christ our Lord, is faithful" (1 Corinthians 1:9). No trial is so great that God cannot deliver us. No pain is so great that he does not bring us comfort. And no situation is ever without God's presence.

This is what the LORD says . . .
"Fear not, for I have redeemed you;
    I have summoned you by name; you are mine.
When you pass through the waters,
    I will be with you;
and when you pass through the rivers,
    they will not sweep over you.
When you walk through the fire,
    you will not be burned;
    the flames will not set you ablaze."

Isaiah 43:1–2

When I said, "My foot is slipping,"
    your love, O LORD, supported me.
When anxiety was great within me,
    your consolation brought joy to my soul.

Psalm 94:18–19

Jesus said, "In this world you will have trouble.
But take heart! I have overcome the world."

John 16:33

My soul finds rest in God alone;
    my salvation comes from him.
He alone is my rock and my salvation;
    he is my fortress, I will never be shaken.

Psalm 62:1–2

The LORD upholds all those who fall
and lifts up all who are bowed down.

Psalm 145:14

My comfort in my suffering is this:
Your promise preserves my life, O LORD.

Psalm 119:50

Jesus said, "My grace is sufficient for
you, for my power is made perfect in
weakness." Therefore I will boast all the more
gladly about my weaknesses, so that Christ's
power may rest on me.

2 Corinthians 12:9

Jesus said, "Peace I leave with you; my peace I give
you. I do not give to you as the world gives. Do not
let your hearts be troubled and do not be afraid."

John 14:27

Cast your cares on the LORD
and he will sustain you;
he will never let the righteous fall.

Psalm 55:22

Whether we face death, discouragement, loss or pain, we can take great comfort in knowing that no sorrow is too deep that God cannot feel it with us. And God wants to help deliver us from it. He wants to bring us his divine comfort.

You, O God, do see trouble and grief;
    you consider it to take it in hand.

Psalm 10:14

This I call to mind
    and therefore I have hope:
Because of the LORD's great love we are not
        consumed,
    for his compassions never fail.
They are new every morning;
    great is your faithfulness.

Lamentations 3:21–23

Praise be to the God and Father of our Lord Jesus Christ, the Father of compassion and the God of all comfort, who comforts us in all our troubles, so that we can comfort those in any trouble with the comfort we ourselves have received from God.

2 Corinthians 1:3–4

God is With Us...
Should We Worry?

This always bothered me...

When the outlook is not good,
we should not worry. We need a
change of perspective to realize that
God sees tomorrow more clearly
than we see yesterday. The future
is completely in his hands!

My flesh and my heart may fail,
    but God is the strength of my heart
    and my portion forever.

Psalm 73:26

Jesus said, "Do not worry about your
life, what you will eat or drink; or about
your body, what you will wear. Is not life more
important than food, and the body more important than clothes? Look at the birds of the air; they
do not sow or reap or store away in barns, and yet
your heavenly Father feeds them. Are you not
much more valuable than they? Who of you by
worrying can add a single hour to his life?

"And why do you worry about clothes? See how
the lilies of the field grow. They do not labor or
spin. Yet I tell you that not even Solomon in all
his splendor was dressed like one of these. If that is
how God clothes the grass of the field, which is
here today and tomorrow is thrown into the fire,
will he not much more clothe you?... So do
not worry, saying, 'What shall we eat?' or
'What shall we drink?' or 'What shall we
wear?'... But seek first his kingdom and
his righteousness, and all these things will
be given to you as well."

Matthew 6:26–31, 33

Cast all your anxiety on God because he cares for you.

1 Peter 5:7

The LORD gives strength to his people;
the LORD blesses his people with peace.

Psalm 29:11

Blessed is the man who trusts in the LORD,
whose confidence is in him.
He will be like a tree planted by the water
that sends out its roots by the stream.
It does not fear when heat comes;
its leaves are always green.
It has no worries in a year of drought
and never fails to bear fruit.

Jeremiah 17:7–8

Search me, O God, and know my heart;
test me and know my anxious thoughts.
See if there is any offensive way in me,
and lead me in the way everlasting.

Psalm 139:23–24

Remember, worry will only tie us in knots. Prayer is the only way to cut short our worrying—to cut those knots of anxiety and care and grant us God's peace instead.

The LORD is with you when you are with him. If you seek him, he will be found by you.

2 Chronicles 15:2

"Call to me and I will answer you and tell you great and unsearchable things you do not know," says the LORD.

Jeremiah 33:3

He who fears the LORD has a secure fortress.

Proverbs 14:26

Do not be anxious about anything, but in everything, by prayer and petition, with thanksgiving, present your requests to God. And the peace of God, which transcends all understanding, will guard your hearts and your minds in Christ Jesus.

Philippians 4:6–7

God is With Us...
When We Need Direction

And I questioned the Lord about my dilemma.

God doesn't mind our questions when we come to him with a seeking heart. God is bigger than any question we can ask. And he often will give us the answers we seek in his Word.

God has a plan for us. He cares about our dilemmas, hears our heartfelt cries and will answer us in ways that will astonish us and fill our hearts with songs of joy.

Your word is a lamp to my feet
   and a light for my path, O LORD.

Psalm 119:105

"I know the plans I have for you," declares the LORD, "plans to prosper you and not to harm you, plans to give you hope and a future. Then you will call upon me and come and pray to me, and I will listen to you. You will seek me and find me when you seek me with all your heart. I will be found by you," declares the LORD.

Jeremiah 29:11–14

Since you are my rock and my fortress,
   for the sake of your name lead and guide me,
      LORD.

Psalm 31:3

Show me your ways, O LORD,
   teach me your paths.

Psalm 25:4

God is With Us…
In Our Decisions

"Lord, you told me when I decided to follow You…"

We all need God's divine power from day to day to follow in his footsteps—to learn the eternal, upside-down, inside-out values of God's kingdom so that we may make decisions based on his character and ultimately share in his glory.

Trust in the LORD with all your heart
and lean not on your own understanding;
in all your ways acknowledge him,
and he will make your paths straight.

Proverbs 3:5–6

The LORD gives wisdom,
and from his mouth come knowledge and
understanding.

Proverbs 2:6

If any of you lacks wisdom, he should ask God,
who gives generously to all without finding fault,
and it will be given to him.

James 1:5

Let your eyes look straight ahead,
fix your gaze directly before you.
Make level paths for your feet
and take only ways that are firm.

Proverbs 4:25–26

Guide me in your truth and teach me,
for you are God my Savior,
and my hope is in you all day long.

Psalm 25:5

God is With Us...
As Our Guide

"You would walk and talk with me all the way."

I saw two children walking together one day, happily exchanging words and glances, laughing aloud at shared jokes. They didn't worry about the cracks in the sidewalk or the bumps in the road, but rather skipped along over them.

God wants our walk with him to be just like that—enjoying his company, sharing together and crossing the rough places on our journey home without the slightest care.

Every valley shall be raised up,
    every mountain and hill made low;
the rough ground shall become level,
    the rugged places a plain.
And the glory of the LORD will be revealed,
    and all mankind together will see it.

Isaiah 40:4–5

It is God who arms me with strength
    and makes my way perfect.
He makes my feet like the feet of a deer;
    he enables me to stand on the heights.

Psalm 18:32–33

"I will lead the blind by ways they have not known,
    along unfamiliar paths I will guide them;
I will turn the darkness into light before them
    and make the rough places smooth.
These are the things I will do;
    I will not forsake them," says the LORD.

Isaiah 42:16

God is With Us...
In Our Difficulties

"But I'm aware that during the most troublesome times of my life there is only one set of footprints."

Ruts and potholes. Shadows and deep darkness. The journey of life can sometimes be very troubling. We stumble and have difficulty following in God's footsteps. We are fearful of the unknown. But God's Word reminds us to trust, to believe, to hope.

God will never let us down. He promises us his strength, his peace, his comfort, and his presence. All we need to do is depend on him, for we can never break God's promises by leaning on them.

The LORD is good to those whose hope is in him,
    to the one who seeks him;
it is good to wait quietly
    for the salvation of the LORD.

Lamentations 3:25–26

When I am afraid,
    I will trust in you.
In God, whose word I praise,
    in God I trust; I will not be afraid.
    What can mortal man do to me?

Psalm 56:3–4

The LORD is a refuge for the oppressed,
    a stronghold in times of trouble.
Those who know your name will trust in you,
    for you, LORD, have never forsaken those who
        seek you.

Psalm 9:9–10

God is With Us...
In Our Confusion

*"I just don't understand why, when
I needed You most, You leave me."*

When faced with bewildering
circumstances we may ask "Why did
this have to happen?" God can help
you with those "Why?" questions.
Though it may sometimes seem that
things are out of control, we can take
comfort in God's enduring promises
and constant presence.

"For my thoughts are not your thoughts,
   neither are your ways my ways,"
         declares the LORD.
"As the heavens are higher than the earth,
   so are my ways higher than your ways
   and my thoughts than your thoughts."

Isaiah 55:8–9

The fear of the LORD is the beginning of wisdom;
   all who follow his precepts have good
      understanding.

Psalm 111:10

If you call out for insight
   and cry aloud for understanding,
and if you look for it as for silver
   and search for it as for hidden treasure,
then you will understand the fear of the LORD
   and find the knowledge of God.

Proverbs 2:3–5

Let us acknowledge the LORD;
   let us press on to acknowledge him.
As surely as the sun rises,
   he will appear;
he will come to us like the winter rains,
   like the spring rains that water the earth.

Hosea 6:3

God is With Us…
As Our Loving Father

He whispered,
"My precious child…"

The Creator of the universe calls
me his child—what a blessing!
As children of God we can trust
that our Father will provide for us.

How great is the love the Father has
lavished on us, that we should be called children
of God! And that is what we are!

1 John 3:1

Because you are sons, God sent the Spirit of his
Son into our hearts, the Spirit who calls out,
"*Abba*, Father." So you are no longer a slave, but a
son; and since you are a son, God has made you
also an heir.

Galatians 4:6–7

Through Christ we . . . have access to the Father by
one Spirit. Consequently, you are no longer
foreigners and aliens, but fellow citizens with
God's people and members of God's household.

Ephesians 2:18–19

I will be a Father to you,
    and you will be my sons and daughters,
        says the Lord Almighty.

2 Corinthians 6:18

You, O LORD, are our Father,
    our Redeemer from of old is your name.

Isaiah 63:16

Praise be to the God and Father of our Lord Jesus Christ! In his great mercy he has given us new birth into a living hope through the resurrection of Jesus Christ from the dead, and into an inheritance that can never perish, spoil or fade—kept in heaven for you.

1 Peter 1:3–4

Every good and perfect gift is from above, coming down from the Father of the heavenly lights, who does not change like shifting shadows.

James 1:17

I kneel before the Father, from whom his whole family in heaven and on earth derives its name. I pray that out of his glorious riches he may strengthen you with power through his Spirit in your inner being.

Ephesians 3:14–16

Grace, mercy and peace from God the Father and from Jesus Christ, the Father's Son, will be with us in truth and love.

2 John 1:3

The Spirit himself testifies with our spirit that we are God's children. Now if we are children, then we are heirs—heirs of God and co-heirs with Christ, if indeed we share in his sufferings in order that we may also share in his glory. I consider that our present sufferings are not worth comparing with the glory that will be revealed in us.

Romans 8:16–18

As a father has compassion on his children,
    so the LORD has compassion on those who
        fear him.

Psalm 103:13

May our Lord Jesus Christ himself and God our Father, who loved us and by his grace gave us eternal encouragement and good hope, encourage your hearts and strengthen you in every good deed and word.

2 Thessalonians 2:16–17

You did not receive a spirit that makes you a slave again to fear, but you received the Spirit of sonship. And by him we cry, *"Abba*, Father."

Romans 8:15

God is With Us…
Always!

"I love you and will never leave you, never, ever, during your trials and testings."

We often make promises we can't keep. God isn't like that. God is faithful and trustworthy. When God promises never to leave us, he means just that. He's not going anywhere!

I am convinced that neither death nor life, neither angels nor demons, neither the present nor the future, nor any powers, neither height nor depth, nor anything else in all creation, will be able to separate us from the love of God that is in Christ Jesus our Lord.

Romans 8:38–39

The LORD watches over you—
    the LORD is your shade at your right hand;
the sun will not harm you by day,
    nor the moon by night.
The LORD will keep you from all harm—
    he will watch over your life;
the LORD will watch over your coming and going
    both now and forevermore.

Psalm 121:5–8

All the ways of the LORD are loving and faithful
    for those who keep the demands of his covenant.

Psalm 25:10

Those who trust in the LORD are like Mount Zion,
    which cannot be shaken but endures forever.

Psalm 125:1

God is With Us...
As Our Strong Provider

"When you saw only one set of footprints it was then that I carried you."

Our problems may seem overwhelming, but God's power is stronger than any obstacle we may face. Since God is our Strong Provider, we can be assured that he is in control of every aspect of our lives. He will prepare the way before us. He will never leave us. And he will provide for our every need.

My God will meet all your needs according to his glorious riches in Christ Jesus.

Philippians 4:19

I can do everything through Christ who gives me strength.

Philippians 4:13

The LORD is the strength of his people,
  a fortress of salvation for his anointed one.
Save your people and bless your inheritance;
  be their shepherd and carry them forever.

Psalm 28:8–9

"I will refresh the weary and satisfy the faint,"
  says the LORD.

Jeremiah 31:25

Jesus said, "Come to me, all you who are weary and burdened, and I will give you rest. Take my yoke upon you and learn from me, for I am gentle and humble in heart, and you will find rest for your souls. For my yoke is easy and my burden is light."

Matthew 11:28–30

With God all things are possible.

Matthew 19:26

The LORD tends his flock like a shepherd:
    He gathers the lambs in his arms
and carries them close to his heart;
    he gently leads those that have young.

Isaiah 40:11

No eye has seen,
    no ear has heard,
no mind has conceived
    what God has prepared for those who love him.

1 Corinthians 2:9

I saw a new heaven and a new earth, for the
first heaven and the first earth had passed away,
and there was no longer any sea. And I heard a
loud voice from the throne
saying, "Now the dwelling of
God is with men, and he will live
with them. They will be his people, and
God himself will be with them and be their
God. He will wipe every tear from their
eyes. There will be no more death or
mourning or crying or pain, for the old
order of things has passed away."

Revelation 21:1, 3–4